THE BEST WAY TO MANAGE

ANXIETY

Understanding Stress Is The First Way To Overcome Anxiety And Panic Attacks. Simple Practices To Implement Every Day. Know And Change Habits That Can Help You In Difficult Times.

HENRY BISHOP

Copyright © 2020

Disclaimer

All knowledge contained in this book is given for informational and educational purposes only. The author is not in any way accountable for any results or outcomes that emanate from using this material. Constructive attempts have been made to provide information that is both accurate and effective, but the author is not bound for the accuracy or use/misuse of this information.

INTRODUCTION

The fear that comes with anxiety can go a long way in affecting one's life. If you are among the millions of adults affected by an anxiety disorder, then you would understand the pains and the development. Anxiety disorder is related to panic disorder; it can affect you mentally, emotionally, and physically. Makes your hearts ponders unnecessarily, and feels suffocating.

You are faced with dizziness, sweating profusely while the mind races — your muscles contract, which renders you trapped. You are feeling crazy or dying at the same time. How terrible can that be?

According to a survey, 14 to 18 percent of Americans and Europeans are affected by anxiety and panic disorders.

You need to understand that you are not alone. The question to ask is, why are so many westerners faced with anxiety today? The greater question now is, how can we conquer anxiety, terror, panic, fear, and worry? Is it possible to conquer this without the use of pills or undergoing a lobotomy? The simple answer is YES. In this book, you will be exposed to the causes and effects of anxiety and panic, the history and analysis of treatment, and enhanced methods to manage and conquer both the physical and mental effects of anxiety. You will learn effective ways to stop negative minds from getting at you via mental nightmares and how you can easily gain your breathing during a panic attack. We will as well be looking at different physical and mental techniques to help you relax, learn about different schools of psychotherapy, and how you can choose a therapist. The important part is that you will get to understand the best ways of identifying early symptoms of anxiety, as this will help you to be reactive.

One important thing you need to know about anxiety is that there are different methods that can be used to treat anxiety. However, you don't have to try all the techniques highlighted in this group; all you need to do is to find what works for you.

Story from a Family Friend

Between the ages of 24-30, he was admitted to a hospital for panic attacks for at least three times. During these times, he saw four different psychiatrists, which prompted him to begin regular sessions with a psychiatrist. He took medications for depression, anxiety, and insomnia. However, he never felt himself and always feel like something is missing, or like he was using extra time on earth, he was living through fear and sadness.

The drugs sometimes work and sometimes and sometimes it doesn't. It works for sometimes, then later the drugs would make him feel worse. He was unable to connect with the psychiatrist he saw, which makes him feel like a lab rat, he keeps taste-testing different concoctions in an attempt to making him feel better, and getting relief from fear and depression.

The greatest help he found was in a psychotherapist he met with for over two years. Despite the different attempts, he has tried to stay out of control of his emotions, the psychotherapist came to his rescue and helped him tackle the foundation of the real problems. This was not done by some unknown Freudian analysis or by carrying out research about his childhood.

She instead focused on the present and getting to the bottom of what he was avoiding in his life and the reasons behind the avoidance. He was able to learn how to evaluate his reactions in different situations, and with this, he was able to understand why he reacts in certain ways. He realized that he had always placed himself under undue pressure. Psychotherapy played a major role in his transformation from a "neurotic mess" to a grounded individual.

Due to the therapy, he was able to discover why he was unhappy about certain things in his life. He began to understand what true happiness means to him. Happiness looks far from him, because he was unable to understand the qualities of what he wanted. After several years, he began to realize and understand what he wanted, and everything started having meaning to him.

You can also find your happiness and live a life you admire, free from anxiety and panic. It's not easy to undergo such treatment, but it is achievable. And what more than you could think?

We will be looking at ways to manage anxiety by defining panic, fear, and anxiety. You will also be given the opportunity to undertake quizzes and personal surveys to evaluate our levels of anxiety and the causes.

Welcome to a new beginning as you are set on the road

to a happy life!

CHAPTER ONE

ANXIETY, FEAR, and PANIC

To have a broad understanding of what anxiety entails, it is essential to analyze the context of the other emotional states that are often referred to or compared. Anxiety is derived from the Latin word "worried" or "distressed." From the English dictionary, it is the "state of uneasiness or tension, which is caused by apprehension of possible future danger, misfortune, worry, etc."

This is quite different from fear, which occurs in a situation where it is warranted; Anxiety is centralized on potential danger. For example, you're having fun in the woods when a bear appears from nowhere and begins to chase you. Your reaction is fear, and the fear at that moment is warranted. If things at your job are not going the way you feel, it is normal to feel anxious about it. It's normal to feel an outright fear when you receive a call from your boss on a Monday morning. If things are overwhelming and stressful, it is natural to feel a sense of panic or terror. There's nothing unnatural about having such feelings. We all feel fear at some point in our lives, and we all have our worries. When anxiety begins to take a larger part of your life by keeping you awake at night, affecting your diet, emotions, and relationship, then it is time to give it a second thought.

Anxiety disorders are psychiatric disorders in which the subject experiences chronic anxiety. There are three major classifications of anxiety disorder, and they are based on the stimuli causing the anxiety. People suffering from this form of anxiety disorder may feel anxious facing their daily tasks, face difficulties making decisions, looks on unfocused and preoccupied. Unlike feeling anxious when you get a call from your boss on a Monday morning, you may feel anxious deciding on what to buy for breakfast. You're more likely to feel anxious about work; however, your sense of worry is not usually grounded in a certain situation; it can only apply when there is no overriding reason to worry.

Panic disorder is a more intensified version of anxiety disorders. A panic disorder is a psychiatric disorder in which the person suffers constant panic attacks. Panic attacks are states of intense uneasiness that can be triggered by stressful stimuli or no stimuli. A panic attack can happen at different places such as work, going on a normal routine, or even on the pulpit while address the people around. Unlike the generalized anxiety, panic attacks are deadly, sudden, and could render someone to be physically paralyzed. They are marked by the following physical reactions:

- Breathing difficulty/or hyperventilating
- Dizziness
- Shaking
- Heart Palpitations.

People suffering from panic disorders usually mistake these symptoms for hearing attacks; hence, panic attacks are one of the highest mental-health related issues for ER yearly. Phobias are disproportional fears of non-dangerous stimuli. Phobias are most times linked to panic disorders and anxiety disorders because these fears occur when we are in innocuous situations. While it is normal to feel terror and begin sweating as the bear approaches your picnic area, it looks irrational for you to go through the same sensations by getting into a lift. That's where generalized phobia, disorder, and panic disorders different from the conventional concept of fear. The person standing in the elevator with sweat in his face feels like there's a bear staring him right in his face, and nothing, including rationalization, will make the sensation go away.

So, what does this mean to you? We will be looking at the various checklists for the symptoms of anxiety disorders. Take your time to fill them out and pay close attention to your results. Some of the treatment options discussed in this work will be more effective for certain anxiety than the others. These questions will allow you to evaluate yourself and help you with the best method of treating yourself.

The Generalized Anxiety Disorder 7-Item Scale (GAD-7)

The 7-point generalized anxiety disorder scale is a screening questionnaire used to evaluate generalized anxiety disorder.

1. The Generalized Anxiety Disorder 7-Item Scale (GAD-7)

Answer the questions in the following test based on the frequency you feel.

In the past few weeks, how often have you been bothered with the problems highlighted below?

1. Feeling anxious, nervous, or an edge.

(a) A few days

(b) Almost every day

(c) More than half a day

(d) I am not sure at all

2. Inability to control or stop worrying

(a) A few days

(b) Almost every day

(c) More than half a day

(d) I am not sure at all

3. Having issues relaxing

(a) A few days

(b) Almost every day

(c) More than half a day

(d) I am not sure at all

4. Being restless and finding it difficult to sit still

(a) A few days

(b) Almost every day

(c) More than half a day

(d) I am not sure at all

5. Worrying too much about several things

(a) A few days

(b) Almost every day

(c) More than half a day

(d) I am not sure at all

6. Becoming easily irritable or annoyed

(a) A few days

(b) Almost every day

(c) More than half a day

(d) I am not sure at all

7. Feeling afraid as if your life is in danger

(a) A few days

(b) Almost every day

(c) More than half a day

(d) I am not sure at all

Interpreting the Generalized Anxiety Disorder 7-Item Scale (GAD-7):

It is imperative to note that this test is to evaluate oneself on generalized anxiety disorder. It is not an actual a replacement for clinical assessment. If you think your anxiety requires the attention of a professional, seek a further assessment from a medical professional.

- Scores that fall between 0-4 means little or no anxiety

- Scores that fall between 6-10 means mild anxiety

- Scores that fall between 11-15 means Moderate Anxiety.

- Scores that fall between 16-21 means severe anxiety.

The Zung Self-Rating Anxiety Scale

The Zung Self-Rating Anxiety Scale was created by William W.K. Zung, of Duke University, to evaluate a subject's quantitative levels of anxiety. The 20-item questionnaire measures the levels of anxiety based on their impact on the autonomic, motor, cognitive, and central nervous systems.

To complete in this quiz, you will need to mark the appropriate answer. The point will be calculated based on the numbers in the boxes when completed;

2. Zung Self-Rating Anxiety scale

Note: The score should be the right description of how you feel or behave in the past few weeks.

1. **I feel more anxious and nervous than normal.**

(a) Some of the time

(b) A little bit of the time

(c) Some of the time

(d) A good part of the time

2. **I'm usually scared for no reason.**

(a) Some of the time

(b) A little bit of the time

(c) Some of the time

(d) A good part of the time

3. **I get upset easily.**

(a) Some of the tie

(b) A little bit of the time

(c) Some of the time

(d) A good part of the time

4. **I feel like my world is falling apart.**

(a) Some of the tie

(b) A little bit of the time

(c) Some of the time

(d) A good part of the time

5. **I feel everything is fine and nothing bad will**

   happen to me

(a) Some of the tie

(b) A little bit of the time

(c) Some of the time

(d) A good part of the time

6. My legs and arm are treble

(a) Some of the tie

(b) A little bit of the time

(c) Some of the time

(d) A good part of the time

7. I am worried about back, neck pain, and headaches.

(a) Some of the tie

(b) A little bit of the time

(c) Some of the time

(d) A good part of the time

8. I feel tired and weak easily.

(a) Some of the tie

(b) A little bit of the time

(c) Some of the time

(d) A good part of the time

9. I feel calm, and I can sit easily.

(a) Some of the tie

(b) A little bit of the time

(c) Some of the time

(d) A good part of the time

10. I can feel my heart beating fast.

(a) Some of the tie

(b) A little bit of the time

(c) Some of the time

(d) A good part of the time

11. I am worried about dizzy Spells.

(a) Some of the tie

(b) A little bit of the time

(c) Some of the time

(d) A good part of the time

12. I feel like fainting.

(a) Some of the tie

(b) A little bit of the time

(c) Some of the time

(d) A good part of the time

13. I can breathe easily

(a) Some of the tie

(b) A little bit of the time

(c) Some of the time

(d) A good part of the time

14. I get feelings of tingling and numbness in my fingers and toes.

(a) Some of the tie

(b) A little bit of the time

(c) Some of the time

(d) A good part of the time

15. I am worried by indigestion or stomach aches

(a) Some of the tie

(b) A little bit of the time

(c) Some of the time

(d) A good part of the time

16. I feel like emptying my bladder all the time

(a) Some of the tie

(b) A little bit of the time

(c) Some of the time

(d) A good part of the time

17. My hands are usually warm and dry.

(a) Some of the tie

(b) A little bit of the time

(c) Some of the time

(d) A good part of the time

18. My face gets blushes and hot

(a) Some of the tie

(b) A little bit of the time

(c) Some of the time

(d) A good part of the time

19. I fall asleep easily and get a good night's rest

(a) Some of the tie

(b) A little bit of the time

(c) Some of the time

(d) A good part of the time

20. I have nightmares

(a) Some of the tie

(b) A little bit of the time

(c) Some of the time

(d) A good part of the time

How can you interpret the Zung Self-Rating Anxiety Scale (SAS):

To calculate your score on the Zung self-rating Anxiety scale, add the numbers you marked together. The total score is between 20-80 points.

- A score of 20-44 points means the normal range for anxiety.

- A score of 45-99 points means mild to moderate Anxiety levels.

- A score of 75-80 points means extreme anxiety Levels.

Social Phobia Inventory (SPIN)

This questionnaire was created at Duke University; it evaluates the severity in a survey based on the statement that is suitable for you.

3. Social Phobia Inventory (SPIN)

Read and understand each statement and mark the option that applies to you in the past week.

1. I am scared of people in Authority.

(a) Few

(b) Somehow

(c) A lot

(d) None

(e) Greatly

2. I am worried about blushing when I see people.

(a) Few

(b) Somehow

(c) A lot

(d) None

(e) Greatly

3. I am scared pf parties and Parties.

(a) Few

(b) Somehow

(c) A lot

(d) None

(e) Greatly

4. I stay away from people talking to people I don't know.

(a) Few

(b) Somehow

(c) A lot

(d) None

(e) Greatly

5. Being criticized scares me a lot

(a) Few

(b) Somehow

(c) A lot

(d) None

(e) Greatly

6. I avoid talking to people or doing things to avoid embarrassment.

(a) Few

(b) Somehow

(c) A lot

(d) None

(e) Greatly

7. Sweating in front of people causes me distress.

(a) Few

(b) Somehow

(c) A lot

(d) None

(e) Greatly

8. I avoid going to parties.

(a) Few

(b) Somehow

(c) A lot

(d) None

(e) Greatly

9. I avoid activities that bring attention to me.

(a) Few

(b) Somehow

(c) A lot

(d) None

(e) Greatly

10. I am scared of talking to strangers.

(a) Few

(b) Somehow

(c) A lot

(d) None

(e) Greatly

11. I avoid having pubic speeches.

(a) Few

(b) Somehow

(c) A lot

(d) None

(e) Greatly

12. I would do anything to avoid criticism.

(a) Few

(b) Somehow

(c) A lot

(d) None

(e) Greatly

13. When I am around people, I do have heart palpitations.

(a) Few

(b) Somehow

(c) A lot

(d) None

(e) Greatly

14. I am afraid of doing things that will attract people watching me.

(a) Few

(b) Somehow

(c) A lot

(d) None

(e) Greatly

15. Looking stupid is among my worst fears.

(a) Few

(b) Somehow

(c) A lot

(d) None

(e) Greatly

16. I avoid people in Authority.

(a) Few

(b) Somehow

(c) A lot

(d) None

(e) Greatly

17. Shaking In front of others is distressing to me.

(a) Few

(b) Somehow

(c) A lot

(d) None

(e) Greatly

Interpreting results from the Social Phobia Inventory (SPIIN):

To calculate your point, add 0 to your answers of "a," 1 point for each answer of "b," 2 points for each answer of "c," 3 points for answer "d," and 4 points for answer "e." The total scores are from 0-68.

- A score from 0-20 means there's little to no social anxiety.

- A score from 21-30 means mild social anxiety.

- A score from 31-50 means there's moderate social anxiety.

A score between

- 41-50 means severe social anxiety.

- A score from 51-68 means very severe social anxiety.

Evaluating your Anxiety

The questionnaire helps you to evaluate the qualitative and quantitative level of anxiety. They give you an actual idea about your anxiety if it's social anxiety or generalized anxiety. However, the questionnaire can't make your anxiety go away. They are other surveys online that focus on other categories of anxiety, which include phobia, panic disorder, agoraphobia, etc. Your evaluation should be reviewed by an authorized healthcare provider such as a psychotherapist; and essential factors to consider before choosing a professional with you.

The next step is to look for the causes of various forms of anxiety, how they affect your mind and body, and the perceptions of anxiety in society. You will be amazed that you are not the only managing anxiety; there are lots of successful artists, writers, actors, scientist are also facing the same challenges. Understanding anxiety will lift your spirits, gives you hope, and inspire you.

CHAPTER TWO

IDENTIFYING THE PURPOSE, CAUSES, AND EFFECTS OF ANXIETY

There are various reasons why lots of people are being confronted with anxiety. The reasons vary from genetic and hereditary traits. We might be faced with anxiety when we get to a certain age even if we didn't exhibit any signs of anxiety disorder, or it may be developed over time.

It is worthy to note that anxiety is a normal reaction to stress. To tackle anxiety, you need to understand those things that are stressing you or draining your feelings.

One of the few reasons why phobias are mostly referred

to anxiety is that phobias involve irrational fear. If you are suffering from social phobias and experience fear when you find yourself in a public place, you might end up developing an anxiety disorder. While some phobias may affect us less in our daily activities, phobias lead to anxiety. For instance, having irrational fears of riding in a Jet may not have many effects if you don't travel. However, if you make a long-distance journey than a road trip, your aerophobia may affect your inner instincts. People who generalized anxiety disorder may also feel anxiety over normal but little worries such as jobs, families, finances, and relationships. When these worries occur every time, it may affect one's sleeping ability, lack of focus, panic attacks, or leads to depression.

Self-esteem also contributes to people suffering from anxiety. Low self-esteem is one of the causes of anxiety. People suffering from low self-esteem may feel anxious when they find themselves in a social gathering, which makes them avoid such gatherings. Someone suffering from other phobias or panic attacks may feel low self-esteem because there are little things to what they can do and what they feel comfortable with.

Anxiety affects one's sense of accomplishment, and if not properly treated, it will lead to depression. The reasons why some people are face with anxiety is because, it is related to a "Fight or Flight," reaction in the psyche. The same way the emotion of fear helps the prehistoric ancestors, which allows us to avoid dangerous situations, anxiety also helps them. People suffering from anxiety today are less likely to die from accidents because they don't like to take a risk. However, the question is, "is safety all you want? On the other hand, do you want more for yourself? If you are tired of living a life full of fear, then you need to start working towards it, regardless of whether the anxiety if genetic, or life experience of from childhood.

How the Mind and Body Respond to Anxiety

One powerful reaction from humans is the "Fight or Flight" reaction. It is worthy of note that the mind is "Mind over matter." When we find ourselves in a difficult situation, the brain and the body pass through various steps of protecting us from giving us strength in overcoming the difficulties. The difference between "Fear' and "anxiety or panic" is the reaction. This implies, your body goes through the same reactions irrespective of the situation you find yourself, either when face with a serial killer or face with a phobia such as flying.

You must have come across physical responses of anxiety and panic. There's no difference in this response when faced with a serial killer. Heart palpitations and an increased heartbeat are common, and are one of the reasons why 20-29% of people in an emergency room are linked to panic disorders. Some symptoms include nausea, chest pain, muscle weakness or clenching, headaches, lower immune system function, and the inability to breathe deeply.

When fears begin to set in, the blood in the brain shifts from the prefrontal cortex which is known to be the rational part of the brain and to the periaqueductal gray area, which is also the responses of survival, this is one of the reasons why "rationalizing" doesn't really work when you want to calm an anxious person down, because there's a limited blood in the logical brain for it to function to the optimal levels.

Anxiety, depression, and panic are also known to be related to an imbalance of the brain chemicals serotonin, dopamine, and norepinephrine. According to some researchers, there's a connection between anxiety and the neural circuitry of the hippocampus and amygdala. According to a survey from the Laboratory of John Wemmie at the University of Iowa highlights the relationship between the metabolic factors of PH (acidity) and the carbon dioxide in the response of fear. The survey also helps to understand that patients with panic disorders are likely to experience a panic attack when they inhale 35% air that contains carbon dioxide. The benefit of this research is that while current medications prescribed for disorders and panic disorders do not cover the acidity aspects. WE CAN. Meditation, yoga and exercise, and other techniques covered in this book can enhance the *Ph* balance of the amygdala by working on the level of carbon dioxide in the brain and the body.

Looking at the various qualities found in people who suffer anxiety, you will find out that anxiety is not the end of the world. The energy poured into thinking about negative things can be channel into positive energy. People who suffer anxiety and catastrophic thinking are creative. They are naturally self-aware and empathetic about others. Some notable positive aspects of anxiety include careful planning, motivation, and function.

What's the best way to turn your anxiety around?

The first thing is to confront your fears. If your fears are affecting your growth, then you need to look for a way to overcome them. This is where your creative mental energy comes into play. We will be looking at ways to turn an overactive imagination into creative expression.

You need to remember, that there are many people before you have suffered the trails of anxiety, and many people have channeled the experiences and emotions to artistic expression. The motivation derived from anxiety has helped politicians, scientists, thinkers, actors, and others to achieve their life goals. In the following section, we will be looking at different people and how they've been able to turn their anxiety to success.

A Portrait of Anxiety: Writers, Artists, and their Success Stories

A large percentage of people who suffer from anxiety in history has succeeded in creative arts. However, it is quite difficult to affirm if these individuals succeeded because of their anxiety or because they learned how to manage their anxiety. We can't underestimate the power of imagination, motivation playing a considerable role in their lives and work. Learning to manage your anxiety may put you in the leagues for talented individuals, and here is a list of people who have suffered from Anxiety or Panic attacks:

- Goldie Hawn

- Isaac Asimov

- John Steinbeck

- Johnny Depp

- Kim Basinger

- Oprah Winfrey

- Robert Burns

- Roseanne Barr

- Sally Field

- Sam Shepard

- Sigmund Freud

- Sir Isaac Newton

- Sissy Spacek

- W.B. Yeats

- Edvard Munch

- Nikola Tesla

- Abraham Lincoln

- Alfred Lord Tennyson

- Anthony Hopkins

- Aretha Franklin

- Barbra Streisand

- Cher

- David Bowie

- Emily Dickinson

There are lots of people who have suffered and learned to manage their anxiety and have been able to overcome anxiety. These individuals have been able to break record and have gone beyond anxiety issues to breaking lots of successful records in the society. Now, we will be looking at ways you can settle down and work on your creativity. In this next chapter, we will be looking at the ways of managing your anxiety and panic attacks, putting different mental approaches into consideration.

CHAPTER THREE

MANAGING ANXIETY THROUGH A MENTAL APPROACH

This chapter covers various approaches to managing anxiety. The first category will be looking at is "mental," which means the mind that addresses the mind's reaction to anxiety. Anxiety affects us differently, both mentally and physically; how you manage, it goes a long way in determining the situation. You can make use of the following suggestion and choose the one that works for your best. You will find multiple strategies that will work perfectly for you.

Psychotherapy: How can this help you?

Trying to choose a psychotherapist can be tough for various reasons. The first problem is the financial challenges. Psychologists, Psychotherapists, and psychiatrists are expensive. We will be looking at the different approaches to therapy and why they are important. We will also be looking at the different resources that can be used to find a suitable and affordable therapist.

My friend's decision to see a therapist was based on several visits after seeing different psychiatrists, which he found disappointing. He thought the doctor didn't care about him; hence he couldn't open up to them. Hence, he kept on going to a different pharmacy, hoping to find a solution with a "medicated cocktail." Seeing a psychotherapist changed his life.

It was a difficult process of self-evaluation and gaining internal courage. Having a therapist is like having an angel, best friend who helps you with everything about your life. Changing a habit comes in four steps: Non-awareness, Recognition, Self-Awareness, and Non-awareness. To have a broad understanding of this, you need to put the following into consideration. Let's assume you realize that you're overweight, and you decide to reduce your weight. In analyzing your eating habits, you will discover that you consume more sugary and unhealthy foods. This implies you've gone from Non-awareness to Recognition of your habit. Self-Awareness is when you decide to change your habits. At first, you feel self-conscious. You are thinking about food at the same time evaluating what to eat and what not to eat. If you're successful, you will begin to be conscious of your diet until you effect the changes. Whereas you're fond of eating bagels and cream cheese for breakfast, now you find yourself eating yogurt ad grapefruit. This shows the second "Nonawareness." At this point, you've reached the habitual change.

Therapy is like a diet change. At the initial stage, you feel self-conscious and uncomfortable evaluating your life, and how you can work things round to make it better. This is the point you begin to experience change. Whereas you often lose your temper and scream over little things and slow yourself down by working on your emotions. You focus on the objectives and find solutions to the problem. This event might have ruined your day before, but now it is a passing moment.

Choosing a psychologist or a therapist to work with is essential than choosing a family home or the best car. If you're pushing yourself to work with someone you don't feel comfortable with, you might end up not achieving your actual goals. That said, there will be times you will feel uncomfortable at the therapist's office. That's part of the work. Finding someone, you can confide in means you can face those moments of discomfort and move through them instead of choosing the easiest way by walking away. To start this journey, we will be looking at the different schools of psychotherapy and their qualities. These lists comprise the mainstream approaches to psychology that you can easily relate with and understand. You need to see this as a car model; you don't just jump in the driver's seat without understanding the engine.

Types of Psychotherapy
Cognitive Behavioral Therapy (CBT)

Cognitive-behavioral therapy is one of the commonly used techniques to address anxiety disorders today. This technique involves focusing on the present situation by dealing with fears and behavioral change. A good CBT therapist will tell you about the things going on in your life, your fears, a problem you're likely to encounter, and how you can systematically change your responses to different stimuli.

Unlike Freudian analytic psychotherapy, CBT is quite different; you are looking at what is happening to you now and not looking at your past experience, childhood experience, finding the underlying causes of the behavior. Here, you are focusing on how you can respond with different approaches from your therapist. One of the reasons why CBT is considered effective is because it involves "exposure therapy." Exposure therapy discusses phobias and anxiety and how to overcome them by exposing the subject to stimulation in a safe environment. It is important that you have a professional that will put you through when approaching exposure therapy. This is not about throwing someone who is afraid of water into the ocean. This is a gradual process of changing the mind's response to stimuli. There are six different stages that cover the cognitive behavioral therapy process:

- Assessment: Being aware of your fears and the effect in your life.

- Reconceptualization: Changing your perception of fear-inducing stimuli.

- Skills acquisition: Developing skills to help you overcome anxieties and fears.

- Skills consolidation and training: Practically using your skills to get effective results.

- Maintenance: Developing habits and maintaining skills that will help you manage anxiety when the needs arrive.

- Assessment Follow-up: Checking and assessing the skills to confirm if they are still relevant and if there is any new development or lapses.

Freudian Psychoanalysis

Many people think of Freudian psychoanalysis when they want to visit a therapist. Freudian psychoanalysis is a broad term; however, there are various methods or techniques under this term. One basic way Freudian psychoanalysis work is that the client-patient visit the therapist to discuss his or her personal dreams, fantasies, thoughts, and free associations. It is the work of the psychologist to interpret these revelations and help to understand the cause behind the revelation. Freudian psychoanalysis works more effectively on anxiety than CBT because it helps to examine the main causes of anxiety, unlike cognitive behavioral therapy, which focuses on the solutions. We have six basic principles of traditional psychoanalysis:

- Personal emotional development is characterized by his/her childhood experience.

- Human behavior and thinking are influenced by irrational drives.

- The irrational drives that serve as motivation for human behavior are largely unconscious.

- Defense mechanisms arise when we attempt to bring an unconscious drive to conscious awareness.

- The conflict between conscious and unconscious (ego and identification) can cause psychiatric disorders such as anxiety, neurosis, panic, depression, etc.

- The ability to free the mind from the effects of unconscious drives is achieved by accepting the conscious mind.

Group Therapy

Group Therapy shares similar features with analytic therapy, cognitive behavioral therapy, and other approaches that guide psychologists. Group therapy involves two or more therapists leading a group of patients through a session together. This is quite helpful as it helps to make us feel we are not alone and helps in easing our minds. Listening to other people's stories can give us motivation and support, unlike one-on-one therapy, which only deals with your own fears. Another benefit of group therapy is, it exposes you to different part stories and how others are managing their fears and anxiety. For example, if you are suffering from social anxiety, group therapy can help you conquer your fears by exposing it to a safe environment. On the other hand, group therapy can limit some individuals because of their fears for social situations that may cause them to participate.

Family Therapy

Family therapy involves both couple therapy and family counseling. One of the benefits of family therapy is that it involves people that surround you and see you every day, and this will help your anxiety, and it's stimuli within the household. Family therapy offers interpersonal support systems, and allows the family to vent their fears, frustration, and motivations. Family and couple therapy enhances our method of communication with our loved ones, and promotes understanding within the family while we work on our anxiety and fear.

Choosing a Therapist

I'm sure you now understand the different categories of psychotherapy and how they work. The next step is how to choose a therapist that will work best for you. Although there is a certain therapy that will work better than others for certain people. However, you need to use a therapist you are comfortable with. If, after working with a one-on-one psychologist and you feel you can achieve a good result more than the group setting, I would suggest you go for it! A good therapist will help you find what works best for you. The next question is how to find a good therapist?

- You can find useful information on The Anxiety and Depression Association of America (www.adaa.org); they have a full page for a therapist that specializes in anxiety and depression.

- You can find a list of therapists and medical practitioners on The American Psychological Association (www.apa.org) and the American Psychiatric Association (www.psych.org).

- You can ask your friends and family referrals.

- Anxiety and other mental health issues may leave you with social stigma; however, you can ask some close friends and family you trust for their sincere advice. If you have someone that's seeing a therapist with a healthy communication with them, you can ask for a referral.

- You ask professionals in your locality if they offer referrals. If your insurance does not cover psychotherapy or any therapists within your area, then look for someone that is not covered.

- Seek for their advice and if they have a package that covers your insurance plan. You can as well ask about professionals that offer a "sliding scale" for payment. A sliding scale here implies that the therapist or their group applied fees is based on your household income. These could help you get a better deal.

- Check the resources at local colleges and universities. You can ask for recommendations if the school offers psychology or psychiatry related courses. They can recommend to people they've trained.

Questions to Ask and How to Assess If You Are With The Right Therapist

Once you find a therapist, make an appointment and consultation. Below is a list of questions to ask the therapist and how to evaluate the therapist upon your first visit.

- History: Ask about the therapist's history, how long they've been in practice. How frequently have you worked with patients suffering from anxiety? What is the status of the clients, and do you still keep in touch?

- Policies: How much do you charge for each session? Are you under any insurance policy, and how often do you work? How frequent are session scheduled? Do you facilitate group sessions or one-on-one sessions?

- Background check: This could be done before or after. It is advisable to check the background of the therapist before commitment. Know if there have been any breaches in professionalism, confidentiality, etc. Has there been any lawsuits that are linked to him and or his work?

After meeting with the potential therapist, then the next question is to ask yourself about the experience:

- Am I comfortable with this therapist, and will I be able to discuss personal issues with them?

- Does this therapist have my interest at heart, or are they engrossed with their notepad, or are they looking at me and evaluating my body language?

- How many questions do they ask? Is the therapist making an attempt to get to know and understand my personal issues?

- Did they establish a goal and did they ask my goals for seeking therapy?

- What are the resources available at the disposal off the therapist? Can group sessions be accepted in the long run if I decide to approach another method? Do they have another technique for couples and families?

- How do I feel their advice about their feelings, aims, and objectives? Does the therapist look capable of helping me?

If you are able to answer questions, then you will be able to decide if the therapist is the right person for you. You need to understand that feelings of discomfort are part of undergoing therapy; however, you need to feel comfortable with your therapist. If you are not comfortable with the first in the consultation or first session, then you can look elsewhere. Finding someone, you feel comfortable and safe with can make a difference between managing and overcoming your anxiety. You need to find someone you can trust, confide in, discuss with them about other techniques you feel comfortable with, and the plans towards implementing anxiety management. Ask questions about other unknown techniques you can try. In conclusion, be grateful for finding a guide to you through the road of fear and anxiety management.

The Essential Structure and Routine

The economic problem has affected the impact of the number of people suffering from anxiety and stress today. There are lots of stress that come with worrying about being jobless, money issues, and lots of people having little or no time on their hands. Some don't know what to do because they've lost their jobs; having no jobs means they have more time on their hands. Some are faced with anxiety because they couldn't; they are not doing what they like. When you meet a good therapist, he or she will be able to detect your fears, because you will be physically and emotionally draining, have issues with your sleep, eating foods you can't imagine.

The Importance of Structure and Routine

When I first saw a therapist because of my debilitating fears, I had almost no structure in my daily routine. I switched from staying in school, from college to graduate school - and in my "real world," it was a disaster. At that time, the security that the school gave me was not clear to me. Even as an active student, my class is based on a solid class time structure, practice time, show time, and so on. Because of the nature of this structure, I drift-free and feel more like an "artist" than a structured "box." It wasn't until the structure was destroyed that I was really nervous and lost myself in a sea of fear.

The transition from college to work is one of the tensest transitions a person has ever experienced in the world today. It might not look like it should - and maybe it was a less stressful event fifty years ago - but in fact, it was your first time entering adulthood. The hope that you will support yourself is worrying, but because college graduates are increasingly confronted with a troubled labor market, this can be devastating.

The number of university graduates who are forced to return with their parents is higher than before. If you are fortunate enough to stay afloat without moving house, I can assure you that nothing can harm the ego anymore. The economic downturn is undoubtedly having a direct impact on the number of people suffering from anxiety and stress now. Aside from the stress of just worrying about money, the unemployment rate means that more people have the extra time they have - a time when they don't know what to do because they lost their jobs or haven't found a niche. No workplace yet. Or, as in my case, they work in a profession that is not in accordance with what they have been taught and does not have a uniform structure. On my first therapy visit, my therapist explained that I was in the east. I'm tired, I have a circle under my eyes, I haven't slept well for months, and my diet consists of some of the worst foods you can imagine.

When my therapist asks about my daily routine, I can't even define it. It's changed too much. I work as an auction bar in Soho, New York, and often end my shift at 4:00 at night. I often do not go home until sunrise, and then sleep until 2:00 pm and go back to work. If I leave or go to bed that day, I am too worried to leave my house, or I will start walking and panic because I don't know what to do with myself. Ironically, I speak completely against the idea of developing a structure for my life. I spent years at the academy and respected my structure, but I didn't know me, and I felt like, "No, no, no. I'm an artist. I'm a New Yorker. This is a city that never sleeps. I won't be throwing walls around you and meeting your strict standards. That's why I moved here! "I never said that out loud, but it made my subconscious cry. I largely ignored my therapist and lived an unstructured, difficult, and stressful life.

What ultimately changed my behavior was the sudden abandonment of everything. This may be drastic and unnecessary, but everyone will arrive at the truth in their own way. That was a total disturbance for me.

My fear is getting worse. I began to feel the walls curve everywhere I went. I fell into the subway, panting in the elevator, and was so afraid of walking on the sidewalk that I just left home to work. Finally, I quit my job and stayed in bed for ten days without food. The only thing that persuaded me to get help was the restless steps of my cat and my grandmother's request to go home.

My experience is not uncommon. They might be too expensive because, unlike the Fresno property market, I tried to get into the world of New York acting, but the feelings I encountered were more general than expected. I think it also makes sense why anxiety symptoms often only appear in the mid to late twenties. There is no doubt that many hopes are expected in this phase of life.

The structure that developed helped me experience the feeling of failure that I encountered when I returned with my family. I continued to "see" my therapist in New York on Skype and see other professionals in my hometown. This time I am more willing to listen to his advice. I tried for a long time to live like a free radical - and that finally made me depressed. I am now ready to adopt the structure.

The structure that I found gave me a feeling of being "free." Instead of seeing it as a set of strict rules, I now see it as a guide, to guide me throughout the day. And it's amazing how you will feel, if you put the basic structure in a life that doesn't exist. Without structure, there is always fear in your mind because you don't know what your plans are. This allows you to feel empowered to move to everything else without worrying.

To Start Developing Structure in Your Life, Below Are The Steps You Need Following:

➢ **Sleep**

We will be looking at the different methods that will help you develop a better sleep routine and how you can work on your sleep schedule. The first question to ask, do you go to bed and wake up at the same time every day? Erratic sleep has been proven to be one of the major causes of anxiety because of the brain's inability to achieve the ideal REM time. You can enhance your anxiety management by working on your sleep routine. You can start by setting you your alarm each day. If you are on a night shift, set it up when you need to get up to start preparing for work. Keep your schedule through the weekend. With this, you will be able to set your "Internal clock" and begin to wake up without the alarm.

> **Morning routine**

The first question to ask, what do you do when you get up in the morning? Do you take coffee? Wake the kids up? Walk the dogs out? Or does this routine weekly? Having a well-structured first hour after awakening will boost your confidence and security before entering the outside world.

- Imagine what your morning would look like if you've carried out everything you're likely to need all through the day. You need to start making efforts towards developing a morning routine that incorporates these things. Another tip is to create five minutes of meditation when you wake up. This will ease your mind and set you up for the day.

- **Scheduling activities throughout the day:** To avoid being overwhelmed with different tasks during the day, it is important to put an effective plan in place before you start. I would advise you to make your schedule the night before the next day; this will make you sleep easier and won't be in bed worrying about your next day's activities. It is not a must you achieve all that you've written down or plan to achieve. You need to be reasonable and be time conscious. You will feel accomplished if you are able to achieve half of what you planned. You can make use of phones and other digital gadgets in planning your day. Some prefer writing, online calendar. Make use of anything you feel comfortable with.

Remember, you're not under any bondage, you are setting guidelines for yourself. Having your day or activities planned out will make you feel less anxious when you unexpectedly arise.

- You can always deal with the present issue and then return your priority list for the day.

➢ **Chores**

How often do you set aside time for basic chores such as vacuuming, dishes, etc. Do you relegate these tasks to the weekend only? If you are able to incorporate these menial activities into your daily activities, the less you will be overwhelmed with the tasks. Spending your entire weekends running errands, cleaning the house could easily drain you, only to return to work on Monday morning, feeling like you never had a good weekend. You can incorporate other activities into your daily activities. Toss the clothing in the washer while you clean up; stop by the market on your way home from work; delegate tasks to different individuals from your family, so you are by all account not the only one trying to get the whole things done.

> **Work**

Work is another place to instill structure; this might look difficult sometimes. When I was doing a menial job, I didn't see the fact that the job was well-structured, but it was. This was one of the reasons why I feel secure at work and less when I am alone.

Irrespective of where you work, home, office, service, you can put in structure in place. This is easier to implement because your job has a clear objective. What is expected of you? How do you go about achieving your goals? The same way you put a plan in place for your daily activities, you can as well you can implement the same strategy in your job. Anytime you are under pressure due to a project, divide the projects and treat them separately. Create a self-appraisal and appreciate yourself when you complete a given task. With this, you will understand that taking little steps go a long way towards achieving greater goals.

➢ **Hunt for Work**

Due to the downturn in the economy, we've seen lots of people lose their jobs, some retrenched from work and some finding it difficult to secure a job. Looking for a job can be overwhelming, which could induce anxiety. This is why it is good to have an effective plan in place. There are lots of places to seek assistance, and you can find helpful tips to help you. There are some local communities that offer job opportunities, skill development workshops, and other great benefits that can give you a sustainable income. You can search online or local newspapers to find jobs or business opportunities. Before meeting your potential employees, you need to take your time to have clear objectives, be calm, relaxed, and surround yourself with positive energy. There are lots of methods that will be discussed in this group to help you reach the state before walking into that office and securing the job.

> ## Family friends and socializing

Are you concerned about the time you spend with family and friends? Does the thought of socializing give you anxiety? Creating a balance in our social lives is an essential element in managing anxiety. People battling with anxiety tend to avoid social gatherings due to the fear of peers or staying around people. However, the support and trust of friends and family cannot be underestimated. They play a huge role in helping us to overcome anxiety and fear. I'm not saying you should jump by entering the club on Friday night or attend galas. You can try to spend more time with friends and family in a social gathering you feel comfortable with. Perhaps, spend a quiet moment chatting with friends, make some cooking arrangements at home, watch movies, or visit a café where you can sit and have a good conversation. Having a healthy social life does not imply that you have to be the talk of the town. It basically means creating a support system for yourself when you are overwhelmed or frightened. Having friends, you share the same mindset with help to boost one's self-esteem. It gives you the opportunity to share your story and share your fears and worries. Share quality time with your friends, laugh as this can help life anxiety.

Chapter Four

Meditation and Its Benefits

Meditation is a conventional practice; however, it has been adopted to help manage anxiety for the past decades. According to research, Meditation is an effective treatment in addressing stress and managing the symptoms of anxiety, phobias, depression, and panic disorder. Meditation is an antidote to breathing dysfunction, and it is an effective way to position your mind, body, and breathe.

We have different schools of Meditation, although the most common and accepted practice is Transcendental Meditation. It offers deep relaxation. Transcendental Meditation was developed by Maharishi Mahesh Yogi and was widely accepted by the western culture in the 1960s and 1970s.

Transcendental Meditation is a form of Meditation that uses a mantra or sound with a practice of 20 minutes, twice per day. Transcendental Meditation does not require any religious activities, even if it was discovered to be part of Hindu beliefs.

Over 600 research has been carried out on Transcendental Meditation, and it has been proven that it improves, emotional, physical, and cognitive effects of stress and anxiety. Looking at these attributes, then it can agree that it's the best option to adopt. Meditation is cost-effective, does not have any side effects, and it is easy to adjust when it comes to managing your anxiety. Looking at these qualities, it will be advisable to consider this option.

How do I Get Started?

There are ways to find a meditation center and instructors in the United States. You can as well check via the local YMCA for information, go through notepad, browse the internet, ask for referrals from friends and family. You don't have to leave the comfort of your home to start the process of Meditation. There are books, audiobooks, videos, and internet resources that can guide you through the process. To start your basic Meditation without a mantra, then you can start with the following process:

> **Find the right time and place**

Give yourself twenty minutes for this session, look go a quiet, solitary, and free form distraction. Turn off anything that can distract you, such as the radio, cell phone, and other devices that could easily distract you.

> **Get into a comfortable position**

People are fond of imagining the full-lotus position when Meditation comes to mind. While this is considered to be an effective position to meditate it is not necessary. You can perform different types of Meditation while lying down, sitting, standing, and walking. For lying down position. Lie on the floor, lay your back flat on the floor. You can use a yoga mat or blanket, depending on your choice. You might be asking why floor and not a bed? You can feel the sensation of your body against the floor. With this position, you can feel your breath entering and leaving your body. Lie with your palms up and your arms by the side. Your legs should be on the floor; if you don't feel comfortable, you can place a pillow under your knees to help balance your bank.

➢ **Close your eyes and relax**

This looks easy, right? There are lots of tips that can help you relax. Focus on your breath. Pay attention to your inhalation and exhalation. It is normal to feel distracted; however, you need to focus on your breathe and let the thoughts go. There's no need to blame yourself or beat yourself over little things. Just focus on your breath.

- **Breathe in through your nose and out through your mouth:** Breathe naturally and pay attention to it.

- **Body detection:** As your breath, allow your mind to detect the different parts of your body. What is the feeling like? What's the reaction of each part of the body when you inhale and exhale? Pay attention to these feelings, what sounds can you hear, and how do you feel about the air around you?

- **Working on the Mind:** Focus on the changes from the body to the mind. What are the things that are having to go through your mind, unconsciously? Acknowledge this thought without criticism, out your efforts into consideration. Now, evaluate your feelings without criticism.

- **Count your breath:** Shift from your mind to your breath. As you do this, begin to count each inhalation and exhalation. Count the inhalation as "1" and the exhalations "2." continue this until you reach" 10." When you have this strange thought, continue from where you stop and don't lose focus.

- **After counting to 10 several times, begin to connect to the world around you:** To achieve this, you need to shift the attention to your body.

Evaluate your feelings and thoughts without self-criticisms. Relax your mind and body until you are ready to move. When you are about to open your eyes, take into cognizance of the sights and sounds around you. That looks easy. However, the paradox of Meditation is that it is both simple and complex. Shutting the mind from external disturbance could be a daunting task. This is one of the reasons why you don't have to criticize your emotions or thoughts during Meditation. If your mind is not settled, make sure you focus on counting. This will help calm your nerves and control your breath and body. Meditation is a powerful tool in managing anxiety, however, it is called a practice for a reason. Keep doing it and don't give up. Dedicate few minutes of your time to mediation and check your stress levels at the end of the week. This will help you know the difference, what has changed in your breathe? Do you feel more relax when you're in a social gathering? You remember that Meditation is an ongoing approach; it may take some time to experience changes; however, you need to keep pushing.

HOW TO STOP CATASTROPHIC THINKING

When it comes to thinking, I could secure a job as the "worst weather forecaster" based on my anxiousness about a disaster. My disaster predictions barely come to the past; however, this has had up and turn to anxiety for years. I have predicted myself into panic attacks, based on my imagination.

The mind is very powerful. We will be looking at how these predictions could have an effect on us. Ron Breazeale, Ph.D. and author of *Duct Tape Isn't Enough: Survival Skills for the 21st Century* defines catastrophic thinking as the worst irrational experience. Catastrophic thinking is the root of many chronic fears. It causes chronic anxiety and can cause panic attacks. Consider the following example to get an idea of how catastrophic thinking creeps and takes control: Your partner is on a business trip out of town for a week. You make a call at night, but on the third night, you call, and no one answers. First of all, keep your mind logical and think that it might be together. But after 30 minutes, when the phone is not answered again, imagine a car accident. You see, the flame of a cargo up and panic. Imagine living together and what it means if you lose that person. They are sure something is wrong. You call again. There is no answer. Your mind is racing. The fire and smoke from this car accident are clearly in your head. Your breath becomes shallow. You start to vibrate. Your heart is racing... Thirty minutes later, your partner called you to say that he is fine and was in a meeting. You are relieved, but you have fallen into tangents. You can't calm down. Mind over matter can be used as a suggestion for positive results, but it can also be the result of disaster thinking. Letting yourself plunge into the worst-case creates physical reactions in your body. These answers are delayed even after your initial fear has passed. They can make you tired, emotionally abusive, and unable to move forward. The only way to stop predicting disasters and engage in catastrophic thinking is to recognize them for what they are and stop them. How do you do it?

> **Identifying**

The mind can sometimes act funny. Catastrophic thinking is usually not announced when it arrives. Like a bad guest, he just sneaks into the back door and blends in with your imagination. When you worry about something for the first time, your mind goes through various results. Sometimes we focus on the worst-case scenario. Why? Our minds do this to prevent disaster. Your imagination shows different results and allows you to decide how you react. Most of the time, the worst-case scenario deviates from logic. You enjoy yourself because you don't know how to react. Listen to your imagination. If you feel like getting into an illogical place, step back for a moment.

> **Replacement**

If you get lost when the clouds smoke in a car accident, stop. To stop your overactive imagination, you need to replace your thoughts with positive ones. Consider different options for the results. Concentrate on the positive. Imagine that clearly. Imagine hugging your partner when he returns safely from your trip. Imagine what you will prepare for dinner when he returns. Imagine you are happy to see them and spend time together. Create a strong and solid image in your mind. If you feel like going back to catastrophic thoughts, focus again on this positive scenario. You can easily be consumed with possible disasters. However, if you direct yourself to this energy to expect positive results, you can be revived in the present. Would you rather look back on your life and find out that half of your time on earth is spent in prison by your thoughts and fears or that you have spent your days completely immersed in it?

To stop catastrophic thoughts require practice, but it can be done. If you can't stop predicting disasters yourself, talk to friends or family members. Sometimes other people's logic can help us put our fears in perspective. For me, catastrophic thinking is something that really helps my therapist. Once I can see thoughts when they arise, it becomes easier to change them. The following technique also helps you stop the negative forecast by putting you on the right track.

Positive Visualization

Positive visualization is similar to the exercise above to protect your mind from catastrophic thoughts. It also contains several factors of meditation. You can use positive visualization as a daily relaxation activity or apply it if you try to prevent yourself from appearing in a void of fear and panic. It works effectively in any situation.

Below is a basic overview of how to start a Positive visualization session. You can change it anytime you encourage your personal growth. The key to positive visualization lies in special features. So take as much time as you need to clearly visualize every detail of your progress!

1. **Start your visualization session in a quiet place without distractions or people:** When you are at home, you can lie down or sit on your bed, on the floor on a yoga mat or blanket. Turn off all cellphones or other interference in the room and feel comfortable. Free your legs and arms and relax your body as much as possible. Close your eyes.

2. **Concentrate on your breathing:** To begin the relaxation process, check your breathing exactly as you want it in meditation. Feel the air when you inhale, and it expands your lungs, lowers your diaphragm, and flows into your stomach. You feel every breath and release of air from your body.

1. **Take a few minutes to focus only on your breath:** When a strange thought comes to the mind, just admit it and leave it. Don't push it. There is no reason to fight with yourself here. Bring your mind back to your breathing and continue.

2. **Concentrate on certain body parts:** Focus your mind on certain areas of the body while breathing slowly and calmly. For the sake of

simplicity, we start with the feet. Take a moment to "come in" with your feet. What sensations do you feel in your toes, heels, and ankles? Do you wear socks? What's the feeling of the materials on your skin?

3. **Breathe in every area of your body:** If you continue to focus on your feet, imagine that your breath exceeds your lungs and extends to your feet. You can stretch your legs and then relax to soften your sensation. Imagine each breath containing healing light. This light enters your mouth, your throat, and spreads throughout your body.

4. **Continue your journey through your body:** After taking a few moments to focus on

your feet, let your mind run-up. Actually, feel the muscles and bones in your ankles, knees, and thighs. Do you feel any tension in any of these areas? If so, just know it. Imagine how your breath reaches this area of tension and how you resolve it. When a bum's mind enters your mind, acknowledge that, and continue. Focus your mind on each particular sensation as you walk through your body. Let your breath stretch your legs, arms, arms, stomach, back, shoulders, neck, etc.

5. **Take a moment before starting:** After going through the process of every area of your body, allow yourself to breathe and relax. Now it's time to visualize! You have just been heated up for

visualization through visualizing your body. We now begin to visualize what you want. There is no "real" preview of what you want. Enough, that alone will make you the happiest, most comfortable, and most peaceful. You can imagine a calm and peaceful environment on a secluded beach. You can imagine that you won the lottery. You can see how you are married or promoted. If the image creates positive feelings, that's fine. You don't have to "perfect" visuals on the first try or even in the fifties - you have more options for imagining different scenarios if you want. For now, leave with your stomach. I have tried for years to imagine the perfect sunset on a tropical island and have never been able to make it work. Then one day, I practiced positive visualization and saw myself bathing puppies. It doesn't make sense - it's a daydream that doesn't make sense - but it works. It doesn't matter if you imagine living in a big house or dancing in a cat field. It is important how clearly you imagine it and how it affects your mind and body.

6. **Create a target:** As mentioned in the introduction, special features are the key to positive visualization. Regardless of whether your imaginative situation is realistic or not, you should really enjoy every detail of the situation. How does the air feel? How cold or warm? What did you touch in your imaginary scenario? What colors can you see? Let your mind explore this

imaginary space and record it all - sights, sounds, smells, textures, and emotions. How does your heart feel in this room? Do you feel at peace? How do you feel?

7. **Slowly return to reality:** Allow yourself to spend as much time in the imaginary place as you want. When you feel ready to return to the world, focus your mind on your breath again. Breathe slowly and deliberately and return to visualize your body. Return from where you started, return to your journey through your body, and examine your arms, legs, chest, back, and legs. When you are ready, open your eyes. Take time to get up and move because some areas of your body can still relax.

8. **Congratulate yourself for creating your own world!** Positive visualization is useful in many ways for anxiety. It promotes relaxation and gives your mind a specific task rather than letting it move chaotically in a circle. Perhaps most importantly, it also helps develop self-esteem. No one, but you created this peaceful environment. You can always come back. It's yours and is specifically tailored to you! Congratulations! Now you have other tricks in dealing with fear, stress, disaster thinking, and panic.

Magazines, Dream Journals, and Creative Outlets

Dreams and nightmares are my indicators of the secret fear that I have in my subconscious, and I have many of them. Even if I feel like my life is going smoothly, there is no better indicator of what is happening deeply than in my dreams. A dream is a time when nothing hinders our imagination from creating and decorating every terrible scenario. I want to say that I have the ability to stop my dreams and instead turn them into positive images, but most do not. However, the next best thing is keeping a dream diary.

A dream journal is useful in many ways. First, they can help calm the rest of the terror that follows nightmares. You do it exactly as your mother or father did when you were a child - they put dreams in perspective. Nightmares don't always make sense, and when you wake up, shiver, and break a cold sweat, don't focus on the "realism" of sleep. You only feel that emotion. But if you stop and burn it, you might find it funny that you are afraid of something as common as a flat tire.

Keep a dream diary in your bed while you sleep

If you wake up in the morning or wake up at night, save it. Give details that you can remember. We lost most of this detail within five minutes of waking up. Because it's important to save them immediately, look back at your dreams later or during the week. See what you notice. Our subconscious not only shows hidden fears from dreams but also clues about what disturbs us in real life. Do you often dream of being mistreated? Or taken on stage without knowing your dialogue? Or do you often dream of finding something that can't be found? This common dream scenario often shows fears or feelings of inadequacy that we don't discuss in our lives. Sometimes this fear seems too big to overcome, so we keep dropping it and hoping to leave. Sometimes we don't know where to start. By analyzing our dreams, we can begin to understand what we fear in our daily lives - and then face this fear.

If you have decided to see a therapist to overcome your anxiety, discussing those dreams in your session can be very beneficial. Your therapist can work with you to interpret the meaning of your dreams and nightmares and to deal with how this fear manifests in your life. If you are working on fear management, dreams can still be a useful marker for analyzing your fears and predicting episodes of fear and / or panic. If I often have nightmares, I know it's time to take a break, step back, and find out what's happening in my life. Then I will extend the time I spend in meditation or see the nutritional changes that I want to make. Knowing that fear is hidden under a blanket, the various methods in this book allow me to do more to create a sense of security and direction.

Public journals are another effective way to control your emotions, thoughts, and fears.

When many people think about keeping a diary, they imagine teenage girls and their pink diary with a small key on the side. There is nothing wrong with this picture, but it is limited. The types of magazines I'm talking about are really personal, but there's rarely a linear story in your life. A magazine is a place where you can save your hopes, fears, ambitions, successes, and even failures. I like to think of magazines as my best mute friends - someone I can tell them all without worrying about repeating, or even judging.

At the beginning of the diary, you might get caught up in various events throughout the day. That's not always bad. If you want to write down how your boss works at the office, that's no problem. But don't limit yourself to it. Allow yourself to write freely. Don't worry if your diary doesn't make sense to anyone but you - that's not necessary. Diary can be filled with bad poetry (or good poetry!), Painted pictures, inspirational quotes, or random thoughts that occur throughout the day. Just express yourself! Journalism must be fun - it shouldn't feel like "boring work." If so, try a different approach. Try to write the page with crap, and then check if you feel free to run and just burn. Writing freely in a diary can help in overcoming anxiety because it eliminates these thoughts and "on the page" where you can evaluate and overcome them.

If you find the journal difficult for you, you can get the same effect from various forms of creative expression. For those who have music, try to capture your thoughts and emotions, and translate them into sound.

If you are visual, take a sketch or tripod and start walking! Your final product does not have to be a masterpiece. You don't need to be seen by anyone other than yourself. Creative expression is a gift in itself. It is also a great tool for changing negative thoughts or disasters and using that energy for something useful. After all, Edgar Allan Poe could have sat in his room and imagined the horror. Instead, he used this emotion to create some of the best literature of his time. Let all the energy in your head develop and be creative!

A quick and effective way to "Trick" your mind the method we have discussed so far in this chapter is the method to increase relaxation, get better self-esteem, and control your fears. This is a method that eliminates anxiety and panic in the long run. But what if you are in the midst of a full panic attack during your morning trip? How do I get back to reality when I'm on a plane or bus and can't find a quiet room to meditate or practice positive visualization? That is about this part.

The following list contains some things you can do if you experience anxiety or panic right away.

1. **Count your breath.**

    Just like in meditation, counting your breath can calm you and focus your mind on the present. You can also count the breaths on a bus, plane, train, or office without focusing on you. Choose a number like "100" to count or count several sets of ten breaths. If thoughts and feelings try to break through, don't judge them - keep counting. Mini positive visualization. As the name implies, this is a "shortcut" to positive visualization that you can experience in public. Instead of lying down and closing your eyes, choose focal points such as door handles or dirt on the floor. It's best not to choose the person you want to focus on unless you want confrontation! After choosing a location, focus your eyes carefully and let your mind estimate a safe and comfortable location. This exercise is most successful if you have already practiced the full version of positive visualization because you already know where to go.

Now let yourself go there and focus on the details of the situation. Imagine the cool sea breeze or the hot sun on your face. When negative thoughts arise, just get rid of it and refocus your visualization. Note: Positive visualization should not be used when driving or operating machinery. This technique is best used for settings such as offices or for travel by public transportation.

2. **Play mental games.**

I have a number of "smart games" that I play when I wait in a long line, take a bus, or in other situations where I am a passive observer and start to feel scared. The aim of the game is to take your mind off the current situation and focus on the thoughts of the apes. One of these games is to trace the alphabet and give a city name for each letter. When you are on a bus, you can count different number plates from other states. Lists are small mind games that are very effective for me because they are simple but require active thinking. Try one or make it yourself!

3. **Write it down.**

Yes, on the subway. Or the bus. Or anywhere. Take out your notebook and write down your thoughts and feelings. Don't judge them and don't scare them - this can only make the situation worse. Instead, just write what comes to mind. You don't have to use punctuation or grammar - just drop it. Physical actions release your fear through words that can often calm your emotions.

4. **Puzzles, games, and other hobbies.**

   Do you like Sudoku puzzles or crosswords? Take these small activities with you when you are in a situation that can cause fear or anxiety. Like a fictional mind game, this activity has the ability to allow your brain something to focus, so it doesn't spin and makes you more anxious.

5. **Call a friend**.

When you are working or even on a bus, you can call a friend using your cellphone if necessary. Sometimes it only helps to hear the voices of people who can be trusted. If you want to talk about your fears, do it - but you don't have to. Just enjoy the comfort of hearing a reliable sound. I even called the therapist when I panicked. That helps a lot.

These are just a few options for dealing with anxiety and panic in an emergency. Most of these techniques work best in relation to the long-term methods described earlier in this chapter. Discuss other options with your therapist about how to deal with anxiety and panic. There are never too many tricks to roll up your sleeves!

The Real Dope on Drugs

Anxiety disorders affect between 14 and 18 percent of the Western population, and there are hundreds of drugs on the market today that target this disorder. There has been an increase in the drug market in the past 50 years to solve many mental health problems, and while these have their advantages, there are disadvantages. Medicines for mental illness have side effects, can cost too much, and can be prescribed incorrectly. Sometimes, they can even worsen the effects of anxiety or depression. If you don't believe me, look for warning signs.

Sometime in the 1990s, the term "Prozac Nation" became a key term in the definition of American society.

This sentence comes from a book of the same name by Elizabeth Wertzel, but it refers to a stubborn "drugged up" state to overcome the trials of daily life. The recipe for Prozac and many of his contemporaries had reached an unexpected level; It has even become "trend" to discuss the pills you have suggested for your various ailments.

The side effects of these drugs and the resumption of "natural and healthy" life have recently begun to change this phenomenon. There are still millions of people who take medication for anxiety, depression, phobias, and other mental and emotional problems. However, if you consider choosing this route; you are far from alone.

The decision to take medication for anxiety, panic, or phobia should be your last choice. Don't go to your doctor at the first sign of anxiety and get drugs you don't know about. In general, doctors should not be your first choice if you want mental health advice. You can prescribe it safely - but are they up to date with research, side effects, and drug interactions? If you have a heart problem, will you see a cardiologist, or will you trust your family doctor's expertise in this particular problem? You must feel the same about your brain. If you have tried in vain for psychotherapy, meditation, positive visualization, yoga, and other therapies in this book, you can consider treatment. The first person to discuss this is your therapist. Although, most psychotherapists cannot prescribe it, they can discuss concerns about various medications with you and can recommend you to a psychiatrist who can prescribe it.

Pharmaceutical therapy is often considered in cases where the patient experiences constant, debilitating anxiety or panic, or when anxiety and depression occur at the same time and cause suicidal tendencies. In both cases, drug treatment and hospitalization are often the standard. Medication isn't always the best answer, but if suicidal thoughts pop into your head, Xanax's side effects may not be that bad! Make sure you have researched and thought carefully about what drugs are recommended. Those who have been on the market for less than seven years often have far fewer research studies. The best method is to look for drugs that have been around for a long time, have been given an adequate rating, and that have obvious side effects and effectiveness.

Chapter Five

Manage fear through a physical approach

Catching your Breath

As discussed in previous chapters, breathing is closely related to our emotions. When anxiety and panic occur, the first clearest signal from your body is the change in your breathing. Just as shallow breathing is a symptom of fear and panic, adjustment can restore your mind from a state of fear. The purpose of breathing is to distribute oxygen from the lungs and throughout the body. When we are afraid, we often hold our breath and hyperventilate. Both actions limit the amount of oxygen our body receives and the amount of carbon dioxide in the blood. Effective breathing techniques, if continuously trained and monitored, can reduce your anxiety and release you from a state of panic. Follow these steps to start breathing:

1. **Lie down or sit in a comfortable position.** When you start this exercise for the first time, it is best to lie down. This is the best breathing and abdominal position when breathing. Obviously, this is not the position you want to use on the bus or plane! We will focus on this arrangement in a moment, but for now, try lying in a quiet place without interruption. Lie down with your hands and feet unbroken and palms facing up while lying on your back. You can use pillows under your knees to stabilize your back and thighs.

2. **Relax.** Lie down for a moment and feel your breath as you enter and exit the body. Your stomach will naturally lift when inhaled and lower when inhaled. People who suffer from anxiety often also suffer from "chest breathing." Breathing in your chest occurs when your chest rises and falls with each breath and your shoulders. This can cause chest tightness and significantly limit the amount of air you take.

3. **Put your hand on your stomach.** Feel how your stomach expands when you inhale. To feel this feeling, try raising your hand as you inhale and lower each time you exhale.

4. **Inhale through your nose and mouth.** Count every breath when you breathe. Count from one to

four when you inhale. Then rest and count to two. Then exhale until you count to eight. Repeat this with your hands on your stomach. Your breasts move slightly when breathing. It's normal. What you don't want is ON your chest. Most of the movements in calm breathing come from your diaphragm.

5. **Practice, practice, practice!** Take all day to focus on your breathing. Take advantage of this reclining exercise when you are preparing to start a meditation session when you wake up in the morning and prepare to sleep at night.

Controlling your breathing in public places is not as difficult as you think. Of course, you will not lie in the aisles at the supermarket and put your hands on your stomach. Instead, you just want to focus on your breath and count your breath and breathe silently. If you are in a situation of worry or fear, stop and concentrate on your breath. Inhale through the nose and count to four, then two seconds, and exhale to eight. Concentrate on your breathing and get rid of thoughts of panic or disaster. Don't be afraid to breathe and concentrate on your breath. With consistent practice, you will realize that you can certainly improve your breathing techniques and control your anxiety better.

RELIEVING TENSION THROUGH STRETCHING AND YOGA

The term "yoga" refers to a number of different practices originating from Hinduism, Buddhism, and Sikhism and originating in the third millennium BC. While yoga is an old practice, little research has been done about its effectiveness in treating anxiety rather than meditation. However, meditation and yoga have a lot in common - especially their focus on breathing.

Further research has been carried out with yoga practitioners in the past decade, and this study shows that yoga is effective in developing relaxation and modulating the stress response system. A 2008 study at the University of Utah showed how yoga affects stress based on how it affects pain. The researchers found that people with poorly regulated stress responses were also more sensitive to physical pain. Because yoga affects the core pain, and their fears are also reduced.

Yoga is also known to improve mood, improve relaxation, improve sleep habits, and weaken the body. All of these are good benefits for sufferers of anxiety. When we feel fear and anxiety, our body reacts with increased muscle tension. Unlike the reaction to fight or run, our body prepares us for confrontation or a way to ease the anxiety. This tension does not disappear once the perceived threat disappears. Instead, it stays in our body and often causes discomfort from pain and cramps.

Yoga practice involves great stretches. Every different positions used in yoga, called asanas or body postures are important. Each of them invites different qualities into our souls. Some asanas have proven to be very effective in treating anxiety by increasing safety and strength. This includes baby poses, forward poses, cat poses, etc.

If you are interested in taking a class to learn yoga, search your local yoga class directory, look for programs at your local university, ask for recommendations from your friends, family, and therapists, and search the web resources if you cannot find a suitable lesson, you also can find tutorials, videos, audiobooks, and even videos online to help you. Yoga is not the only mind-body technique. You may also be interested in tai chi, self-hypnosis, or biofeedback. All of these techniques can help release this great tension from anxiety and give you a better and more relaxed mindset.

Sports and Exercise

If you don't have access to yoga classes and don't want to try it yourself, you can, of course, participate in a number of sports and exercises and still help focus your mind and body. Aerobic exercise expands your heart and helps you balance chemicals in your brain and body. Non-aerobic stretching can help relieve muscle tension and increase relaxation.

So which exercise did you choose? It doesn't matter what sport or non-competitive activity you enjoy. Why not competitive? Because non-competitive activities reduce stress. You may enjoy playing football, but top-tier sports often cause stress rather than diminish it. So choose something that is soothing, and you can introduce yourself or in groups. Examples of these activities include hiking, walking, jogging, biking, swimming, kayaking, skiing, and mountain climbing. Whatever you choose, enjoy, and the benefits will come. You will feel more inspired, calmer, and more balanced.

Sleep and Relaxation Techniques

In this book, we discuss aspects of sleep because sleep is an important factor that influences and causes fear. This can be a vicious cycle: you feel anxious and cannot sleep. Your lack of sleep, in turn, causes more fear and emotional fragility. Is there a way out? No doubt. There are many.

Most of the methods in this book are related to sleep in a number of ways. Meditation improves sleep quality and physical activity, such as sports and yoga. Better breathing even improves sleep quality. Creating a sleeping routine helps. But what if all this isn't enough? How can you get the rest you need to keep your mind and body healthy and anxious? First, make sure your bedroom is free of distractions.

Your bedroom must be a room in the house that is only provided for rest and relaxation. There is no television, radio, smartphone, or computer staring at you when you rest. If your alarm clock is a function of your cell phone, make sure that this is the only reason why this is used in the bedroom.

Second, establish a solid bedtime routine. Wait for an hour to get ready for sleep and go to work, family anxiety, and other torturous thoughts during this time.

Take a warm bath to increase relaxation. You can light

a scented candle, which also has a calming effect. Don't

do any tasks at this time. Relax!!

Third, when you go to bed, bring a good book or maybe

a crossword. Don't record an interesting novel that you

can't write, but take something more entertaining.

Inspirational books and self-help books are great to read

when you sleep, as long as they don't wake you up and

worry about what problems you might have. Finally,

make sure the room is dark, quiet, and peaceful. If, for

some reason, you wake up and can't sleep, write a diary,

or even breathing exercises. If your concern keeps you

awake, write it down - and let it go. The better you sleep,

the better you will feel the next day and overcome your

fears.

Food and Nutrition

The final aspect that we will see in the physical approach to overcoming anxiety is nutrition. According to a recent study published in the American Journal of Psychiatry, food and nutrition can have a significant impact on stress and anxiety levels. In the study, researchers tracked the eating habits of more than 1,000 women for ten years. The results showed that those who ate fast food, processed cereals, cakes, beer, and processed foods were more likely to experience depression or anxiety than those who ate healthier than unprocessed vegetables. Meat and seeds.

It might be obvious to eat healthier, but some foods can actually change the balance of chemicals in the brain and affect mood. The following is a list of some of these foods and how they affect brain chemistry. Vitamin B. Vitamin Group B plays an important role in cell metabolism and includes the following: thiamine, riboflavin, niacin, pantothenic acid, pyridoxine, biotin, folic acid, and cyanocobalamin. The following foods are rich in B vitamins and folic acid:

- Asparagus

- Cabbage

- Bananas

- Oranges

- Peaches

- Chicken giblets

- Kidney

- Egg yolks

- Beans

- Lentils

- Peas

- Liver

- Soy products

- Nuts

- Wholegrain bread

- Potatoes

- Spinach

Omega-3 fatty acids: These fats are often found in vegetable and animal oils. Bad omega-3 fatty acids can cause depression and anxiety, according to several studies. Conversely, several studies have found that an increase in omega-3 fatty acids can correct this problem.

Foods high in omega-3 fatty acids include:

- Sardines

- Flax seeds

- Walnuts

- Grass-fed meats

- Salmon

Inositol: Inositol is a compound found in many foods that the body uses in several serotonergic and cholinergic receptors. Inositol can be found in:

- High-bran cereals

- Nuts

- Beans

- Cantaloupes

- Oranges

Other foods that help overcome anxiety: Other foods that help overcome anxiety are whole grains with the high magnesium content. Whole grains also contain tryptophan, which is converted to serotonin in the body.

Serotonin is a neurotransmitter that promotes feelings of calm and happiness. Algae are also rich in nutrients and have a high magnesium content. Blueberries are considered "superfoods" because they are so rich in vitamins, phytonutrients, and antioxidants. Peaches have properties and benefits similar to blueberries. Acai Berry recently won the superfood category. Acai berries are rich in phytonutrients (also blueberries) and contain lots of antioxidants. Dark chocolate has many advantages, and several studies have shown that dark chocolate (without the addition of sugar or milk) reduces stress and creates a feeling of calm.

Eating healthier foods has many benefits to relieve stress and anxiety so that the body stays balanced and healthy. Eating healthier can also help you sleep better. However, keep in mind that the opposite is true for foods loaded with saturated fat, caffeine, and alcohol. Foods and drinks that are commonly consumed can increase anxiety, insomnia, and decrease cognitive function. Eat well, sleep well, and feel good!

CHAPTER SIX

ALTERNATIVE METHODS FOR TREATING ANXIETY

In this chapter, we will look at some traditional methods that you can use to deal with anxiety and stress. These methods are less scientifically researched than the techniques presented so far, but they are recognized by many people who face the daily struggle of anxiety. Discuss important diet changes or take herbal medicines with your doctor before continuing, because he can tell you about health or drug interactions. These methods, combined with previously introduced techniques such as meditation, yoga, and eating, can significantly improve your mood and create a more peaceful, happier life!

Aromatherapy refers to the ancient practice of using flavor essential oils to ease one's mood. Aromatherapy, now considered a form of "alternative medicine," can be effective in treating anxiety by creating a relaxed atmosphere of relaxation. In fact, aromatherapy is always used. When you think about it: we use perfume, soap and scented shampoo, air freshener, and scented candles without thinking about it. Why do we use this product? Because, of course, it smells good! Despite the lack of research to support aromatherapy as alternative medicine, it is difficult to deny the pleasant fragrant qualities for mood and senses.

You can buy essential oils at grocery stores, herbal stores, or online. However, you don't have to limit yourself to essential oils. If you find a scented candle that you like, use it! Aromatherapy is perfect for calming baths, meditation sessions, and visualization sessions - as long as you are well-ventilated, so you don't become overweight! The following list contains essential oils that are known to provide a soothing fragrance, and are recommended for people with anxiety:

1. **Ylang Ylang:** Ylang Ylang is an essential oil extracted from the flower of a plant known as the "perfume tree." Besides anxiety, ylang-ylang is used as an essential oil to relieve hypertension and normalize skin problems. This is an amazing ingredient from Chanel No. 5, so it can't be said that

"Eastern Mystics" appreciate the aroma of the Ylang Ylang flower. Calming effect, this oil helps relieve stress.

2. **Bergamot**: Bergamot is an essential oil from the orange bergamot tree, which grows in southern Italy and France. Bergamot is often used in Earl Gray tea - another example of "aromatherapy" used in the main product. The smell of bergamot is orange and raised; this works well to calm the nerves.

3. **Sandalwood** comes from sandalwood, which is harvested and cut and has been used as an essential oil for centuries. It has been used mainly in the religious rituals of many Chinese, Indian, and

Japanese religions. It has a musky, woody fragrant and has a calming effect on the nervous system.

4.   **Chamomile.** Not just for tea! Chamomile has a sweet and slightly fruity fragrant and comes from Roman chamomile flowers. If that happens in the garden, you should consider growing chamomile because the aroma really brightens the garden! Chamomile flowers can be broken down into tea or distilled into essential oils. Chamomile oil and chamomile tea are ideal for calming the mind and reducing stress.

5.   **Lavender:** Lavender has been linked to stress relievers for years. Lavender comes from the mint family and grows throughout the world. It can be used in food, tea, and essential oils. Lavender is a

popular stress scent that is usually found in scented candles, bath salts, and perfumes.

6. **Geranium rises**: This is another flower commonly used in the perfume industry, healthy roses, is mostly planted for refining in South Africa because of its oil. Geranium Rose is ideal for creating a calming atmosphere and is also used to balance hormones.

These are just a few of the essential oils that are commonly used to treat anxiety and stress. If you enjoy aromatherapy, I highly recommend that you investigate further and find more scents that will give you a better feeling of calm and relaxation.

Hypnotherapy

Hypnotherapy includes Hypnosis, as the name suggests. Dr. John Capas, the founder of the Hypnosis Motivation Institute, defines the role of a hypnotherapist as follows: "Causing the hypnotic state of the client to increase motivation or changing behavior: contact the client to determine the nature of the problem. This prepares the client to enter the hypnotic state by explaining how Hypnosis is functioning and what the client will experience. Tests to determine the level of physical and emotional suggestion. Individual hypnosis methods and techniques based on interpreting test results and analyzing client problems can train clients in self-hypnosis.

Hypnotherapy can be used to overcome the basic fears and fears it causes. At the same time, like cognitive behavioral therapy, this is also used as an initial approach to exposure therapy. Nowadays, hypnotherapy is often used to manage and support anxiety, depression, phobias, insomnia, and addictions. To find a certified hypnotherapist, check online, ask a friend for help, and discuss this method specifically with your therapist. He can recommend a hypnotherapist, or at least discuss the pros and cons of this form of therapy.

Acupuncture

Acupuncture originated in ancient China and involved the use of small needles inserted into acupuncture points on the skin. The reason for acupuncture is to release the energy stored in the body's meridians, thereby creating balance. Current scientific studies show that traditional acupuncture effectively reduces pain and nausea. Although studies do not categorically show the effectiveness of acupuncture in relieving anxiety, many patients have found this practice useful. If you are interested in testing the benefits of acupuncture, make sure you do adequate research on your doctor. Acupuncturists in the United States must participate in an accredited program and have a license for 3-4 years. Fake acupuncturists, like fake chiropractors, can do more harm than good. Make sure your acupuncturist is qualified, has a satisfied patient history, and is licensed.

CONCLUSION

Anxiety is a very common disease in our society today, and there are many reasons for it. The change in the way of life of Americans – and even globally - has changed the way the mind sees and handles stress. Stress is a normal part of life - we are told. Over the past fifty years, Westerners have fundamentally improved the way we work, play, socialize, and maintain well-being. Change is not always a bad thing, but it can cause concern. Until we learn to adapt to a world full of smartphones, to surf the Internet, television, and ceiling advertising in any form, we will feel anxious.

Transitions in society cause fear, as does change in individual lives. If you face marriage and a commitment to life, you will feel anxious. If you have children, you will feel anxious. But what about the fact that work has changed exponentially since 1950? It is unreasonable to hope that people will not care if their profession has progressed from the assembly line to the computer development laboratory. People and society expect different things from us today - and this can cause fear. Saying that you are afraid does not mean acknowledging personal failure. Fear is normal in the face of a constantly changing world.

How you deal with this fear is very important. Anxiety management means the difference between fear of leaving home or facing everyday problems and living a healthy, satisfying, and peaceful life. This means that if you experience problems, you can experience and fix them instead of running them.

Use the methods in this book to create your own calm atmosphere in a storm. If you take a few moments, you can concentrate your mind and body effectively. This way, you can truly appreciate your friends, family, and the world around you never like before. Living your own life path without fear can include working with a therapist or just learning to plan your time effectively. If you are like me, this can involve different techniques, if you know what works. Whatever you need, you owe it to yourself. You deserve to live a happy, fearless, down to earth life!